PREMCHAND

THE SALT INSPECTOR
EIDGAH

First published by Westland Books, a division of Nasadiya Technologies Private Limited, in 2024

No. 269/2B, First Floor, 'Irai Arul', Vimalraj Street, Nethaji Nagar, Alapakkam Main Road, Maduravoyal, Chennai 600095

Westland and the Westland logo are the trademarks of Nasadiya Technologies Private Limited, or its affiliates.

This comic is an adaptation of two short stories by Premchand— 'Eidgah' and 'Namak ka Daroga' (The Salt Inspector)

ISBN:

10 9 8 7 6 5 4 3 2 1

Comic Script: Anurag Kumar Singh and Athiyan Arumugam
Art and Corrections: Ayushi Anand, Rashmita Narayana, Pankaj Deore and Tanisha Tiwari
Lettering: Pooja Padmashali
Art Direction: Giridharan Vasu and Mahesh Sharma
Creative Quality Control: Abhigyan Singh
Creative Producer: Rajeev Tamhankar
Book design by New Media Line Creations, New Delhi

Printed at Parksons Graphics Pvt. Ltd

THE SALT INSPECTOR

Uh!
Munshi-ji
I heard that a job posting has been issued in the salt department for a salt inspector's position.
Yes, I heard that too.
Have you thought of giving it a try?
Me? How could I possibly become an inspector?
It's people like you, who read romantic and erotic literature in Persian, who manage to secure prestigious positions these day.
Why not, brother? You are well-educated and proficient in Persian.
I believe that fortune is at your doorstep, Munshi-ji. Seize the opportunity.

When a new department was set up to prohibit open salt trade, people began to engage in illicit trade.
They employed all kinds of devious methods. Some tried bribery, while others turned to smuggling.
Government officials had a field day. People abandoned the universally respected role of the patwari and sought positions in the salt department.
Even lawyers aspired to become salt inspectors.

Your family is going through a difficult time. But once you become an inspector, all your worries and hardships will vanish.

Should I give it a try?

My son, you know what our situation is like. We are under heavy debt, and the young girls in the family are growing up so quickly, like weeds in the field.

I'm like a tree on the edge of collapse. Now, you're the master and head of the family.
Don't bother with status in a profession; it's like a Pir Ka Mazar. Your focus should always be on the offerings, the chadhawa and the chadar.

Look for a job that offers the opportunity to earn extra income on the side.
A monthly salary is like a full moon – shining brightly for a day, but gradually waning until it disappears.

An illicit income flows like a never-ending stream, continuously satisfying your needs.
A salary, being man-made, has limitations and may not take you very far. But an additional income source is a divine gift that paves the way to prosperity.

You are a scholar yourself and require no further guidance. Rely on your own knowledge and judgement.
Consider the needs of people, the opportunities, and then make the decisions you believe are best.

Yes, Father!

MUNSHI VANSHIDHAR SOUGHT HIS FATHER'S BLESSINGS AND EMBARKED ON HIS JOB SEARCH.
HE POURED BOTH HIS PHYSICAL AND MENTAL EFFORTS INTO THIS OPPORTUNITY.
OVERCOMING EVERY CHALLENGE, EVERY OBSTACLE.

THROUGH UNWAVERING DEDICATION, MUNSHI VANSHIDHAR ACHIEVED HIS GOAL.
Welcome to the Salt Department, Munshi Vanshidhar. I have confidence in your commitment and integrity.
I will never let you down, sir.
AND THAT IS HOW MUNSHI VANSHIDHAR SECURED THE JOB OF AN INSPECTOR IN THE SALT DEPARTMENT, BOASTING OF A HANDSOME SALARY.

WHEN THE NEWS REACHED HIS FATHER, HE WAS VERY HAPPY.
Well done, Son! Today, thanks to you, your father's head is held high. I can now proudly declare that I am the father of an inspector.
It's all thanks to your blessings, Father.
MUNSHI VANSHIDHAR EMBARKED ON HIS DUTY WITH UNWAVERING DEDICATION AND HONESTY.
Check this bag properly!
IN JUST SIX MONTHS, MUNSHI VANSHIDHAR HAD WON THE ADMIRATION OF ALL HIS SUPERIORS THROUGH HIS EFFICIENCY AND IMPECCABLE CONDUCT.
Well done, Vanshidhar! Your performance is commendable. The department is proud of you.
Thank you, sir!
THE FAMILY'S LIVING CONDITIONS HAD IMPROVED SIGNIFICANTLY. EVERYTHING WAS GOING WELL.

ONE WINTER NIGHT, VANSHIDHAR WAS SLEEPING IN HIS OFFICE.
THE TRANQUIL YAMUNA RIVER LAY ABOUT A MILE FROM HIS OFFICE, CONNECTED BY A SERENE WOODEN BRIDGE.
Hurrh! Hatt!
Muuuuuuuu!
Clap! Raw!
Hey! Where is that noise coming from?
THE SOUND SHATTERED HIS SLUMBER IN AN INSTANT.
HE GOT UP TO GO.

MUNSHI VANSHIDHAR GOT READY AND PICKED UP HIS FIREARM.
I'm going to investigate.
HE WENT TO FETCH HIS HORSE, GAGAN.
Come on, Gagan! Our duty calls.
GAGAN WAS VANSHIDHAR'S FAITHFUL COMPANION.

THERE WAS DEAD SILENCE FOR A WHILE. FINALLY, A CARTMAN REPLIED IN A FEARFUL VOICE.

It belongs to Pandit Alopidin, sir!
Pandit Alopidin?
Who's Pandit Alopidin?
He is from Daatagunj.
Pandit Alopidin is the most respected landlord in the region. He oversees a business worth lakhs of rupees.
Hmmm. So why does he need to transport secret cargo in these bullock carts in the dead of night?

Where are the carts headed to?
Kanpur.
What are you carrying in these bags?
Uhh ... umm ... it has ...
Why are you stammering like this? Tell me clearly, what is in these bags?
Are you all mute? Tell me what's on these carts.
BUT THERE WAS NO ANSWER. EVERYONE STOOD STILL LIKE FIGURES OF STONE.

Looks like I'll have to check it myself.
MUNSHI VANSHIDHAR MOUNTED THE BULLOCK CART.
HE TOOK OUT A KNIFE ...

... AND RIPPED OPEN A BAG.
So, my suspicion proved to be correct!
Indeed, this is salt.

PANDIT ALOPIDIN WAS FOLLOWING THE CONVOY IN HIS WELL DECKED-OUT CHARIOT.
MASTER! MASTER!
HE WAS HALF ASLEEP AND HALF AWAKE.
Hmm!
SUDDENLY, A GROUP OF RATTLED CART DRIVERS ARRIVED AND WOKE HIM UP.
MASTER! MASTER! WAKE UP!

What happened? Why are you shouting like this?
Master! The inspector has stopped the carts.
He's at the river bank and has summoned you.
Why are all of you so worried? After all, he is just an inspector not a dacoit.
Listen! I have unshakeable faith in Goddess Lakshmi. She doesn't just reign on Earth; her presence is felt even in heaven.

This is the plain truth. Justice and policy, both of these are but the playthings of Lakshmi.
She can make them dance to any tune.
HE THEN ADDRESSED THE CARTSMEN WITH GREAT CONFIDENCE.
Go, I'm coming.

WHEN THEY HAD LEFT, PANDITJI NONCHALANTLY ROLLED A PAAN.
THEN HE COVERED HIMSELF IN A QUILT.
AND WALKED TOWARDS THE INSPECTOR.
Ram, Ram, Daroga sahib! Tell me, what mistake have I made that the carts have been stopped. Show some compassion to us Brahmins.
Government orders!

Did you hear me tell a joke?
No! No! Sir, you told no joke. Sorry! But I couldn't help but laugh at your comment.
Government order? Hahaha!
We don't know 'the government order', or any government. For us, you're the government.
Excuse me?

It's all between us, a family affair. We are not outsiders! You needn't have taken this trouble.
It's impossible that we would pass this way and not make an offering to the god of this ghat. I was just coming to present myself before you.
VANSHIDHAR REMAINED UNTOUCHED BY THE ALLURING MELODY PLAYED ON THE FLUTE OF WEALTH. BEING NEW TO HIS POSITION, HE WAS RIDING THE CREST OF HONESTY.
I am true to my salt, not for sale for a few coins! You're under arrest now.

You will be issued a legal challan. I cannot afford to waste any more time.

Jemadaar Badlu Singh, take Pandit Alopidin into custody and bring him along. This is my order.

PANDIT ALOPIDIN WAS TAKEN ABACK UPON HEARING MUNSHI VANSHIDHAR'S ORDERS.

EVEN THE CART DRIVERS' JAWS DROPPED IN ASTONISHMENT.

THIS WAS THE FIRST TIME EVER THAT PANDITJI HAD ENDURED SUCH RUDE TALK.
BADLU SINGH MOVED FORWARD, BUT HE LACKED THE COURAGE TO HOLD PANDITJI'S HAND.
Now, this is new. Dharma insults artha, morality over materialism! This inspector is rude and unmannerly, but has not yielded to temptation yet.
He is young and hesitant. Perhaps I should handle him in a slightly different manner.

Babu sahib, please don't do this. I'll be ruined. My reputation will be tarnished. What will you gain by humiliating me? I am no stranger to you, surely?
I don't want to hear this kind of talk.
THE GROUND THAT ALOPIDIN BELIEVED WAS SOLID SUDDENLY SEEMED TO BE SLIPPING AWAY BENEATH HIS FEET.
BOTH HIS PRESTIGE AND HIS WEALTH HAD TAKEN A SEVERE HIT, YET HE REMAINED UNWAVERING IN HIS BELIEF IN THE PERSUASIVE POWER OF WEALTH.
Lalaji, please offer one thousand rupees to the sahib. He's behaving like a hungry lion.

PANDITJI WAS FRUSTRATED BY THE UNYIELDING NATURE OF DHARMA. THIS LEVEL OF RENUNCIATION WAS RARE EVEN AMONG GODS, HE THOUGHT. BOTH FORCES WERE NOW ENGAGED IN A BATTLE.
Take five thousand.
Forget one thousand, even one lakh will not veer me away from the path of truth.
ARTHA BEGAN TO PUSH LARGER NUMBERS INTO THE ATTACK.
Ten thousand.
No!
Okay, fifteen.
I said, no!
How about twenty thousand?

BUT DHARMA, WITH ITS EXTRAORDINARY COURAGE, REMAINED UNYIELDING, LIKE A MOUNTAIN, AGAINST THIS OVERWHELMING NUMERICAL FORCE.
I can't go beyond this. You may do as you please.
There's no chance! You are wasting your time.
Badlu Singh! What are you waiting for? Arrest him!
BADLU SINGH ADVANCED TOWARDS PANDIT ALOPIDIN, CURSING THE INSPECTOR IN HIS HEART.
Babu sahib, for god's sake, have mercy on me. I'm willing to resolve the matter for twenty five thousand.
It's impossible.

IT SEEMED DHARMA HAD TRIUMPHED OVER ARTHA. ALOPIDIN WITNESSED A FORMIDABLE FIGURE APPROACHING HIM WITH HANDCUFFS IN HAND.

PANDIT ALOPIDIN LOOKED AROUND HELPLESSLY WITH PLEADING EYES. THEN HE FAINTED AND FELL TO THE GROUND.

THE WORLD WAS ASLEEP, BUT THE TONGUE WAS WAGGING.

BY MORNING, THE STORY HAD SPREAD EVERYWHERE. IT WAS ON EVERYONE'S LIPS, THE YOUNG AND OLD ALIKE.

THE FOLLOWING DAY, PANDIT ALOPIDIN WAS ESCORTED TO THE COURT BY CONSTABLES. HIS HEART WAS HEAVY WITH REMORSE AND ANGER, AND HIS HEAD HUNG IN SHAME.
THE ENTIRE CITY SEEMED RATTLED BY THE INCIDENT. THERE WAS MORE SCRUTINY IN PEOPLE'S EYES THAN THERE WERE PEOPLE IN A BUSTLING FAIRGROUND. ROOFS AND WALLS SEEMED TO MELD WITH THE THRONGS OF ONLOOKERS.

EVERYBODY WAS DISCUSSING PANDITJI'S BEHAVIOUR. CONDEMNATION POURED IN FROM ALL DIRECTIONS, AS IF THE WORLD HAD FINALLY BEEN PURGED OF SINNERS AND SINS.

THE MILKMAN WHO ADULTERATED MILK, OFFICIALS WHO MADE FALSE ENTRIES IN THEIR DIARIES ...
BABUS WHO TRAVELLED TICKETLESS, MONEYLENDERS AND TRADERS WHO FABRICATED FRAUDULENT DOCUMENTS—ALL OF THEM SHOOK THEIR HEADS IN DISAPPROVAL, AS IF THEY WERE THE GODS THEMSELVES.

BUT THE MOMENT PANDIT ALOPIDIN REACHED THE COURT ...
... THE OFFICIALS WERE HIS DEVOTEES, THE JUNIOR STAFF HIS MINIONS, THE LAWYERS HIS OBEDIENT SERVANTS, THE ORDERLIES, PEONS AND WATCHMEN HIS VOLUNTARY SLAVES.
HE SEEMED LIKE THE LION OF THIS IMPENETRABLE JUNGLE.
THE MOMENT PEOPLE SAW HIM THERE, THEY RAN TOWARDS HIM FROM ALL DIRECTIONS.

THEY WERE ASTONISHED, NOT ABOUT ALOPIDIN'S ACT, BUT BY HOW HE HAD ALLOWED THE HAND OF THE LAW TO GRAB HIM.
Seth-ji! I can't believe you are here.
How did all of this come to be?
How could a person with your vast resources and remarkable ability to talk your way out of anything get caught like this?
This is a terrible turn of events! I'm so sorry to see you here.

AN ARMY OF LAWYERS WAS ASSEMBLED TO FIGHT THE IMPENDING BATTLE. IN THE BATTLEFIELD OF JUSTICE, DHARMA AND ARTHA STOOD OPPOSED TO EACH OTHER.
MUNSHI VANSHIDHAR STOOD THERE, SPEECHLESS. HE POSSESSED NO STRENGTH OTHER THAN THE TRUTH AND NO WEAPON EXCEPT THE BARE FACTS.
THERE WERE WITNESSES, BUT THEY FLIP-FLOPPED DUE TO GREED.
Pandit Alopidin is not at fault.
Munshi Vanshidhar orchestrated all of this to entrap him.

VANSHIDHAR HAD THE DISTINCT IMPRESSION THAT EVEN JUSTICE HAD ABANDONED HIM.
JUSTICE AND PARTIALITY ARE INCOMPATIBLE. IN THE PRESENCE OF PARTIALITY, JUSTICE STANDS NO CHANCE. THE TRIAL CONCLUDED SWIFTLY.
The evidence presented against Pandit Alopidin is false and misleading. He is a prominent person. It is unimaginable that a person like him would break the law for such a small gain.
Although Inspector Vanshidhar is not to be blamed too much, yet, his brazen and thoughtless act has caused needless agony to an honourable man.
We are happy that he is watchful and alert in performing his duty, but his overzealousness has destroyed his reason and judgement. He should be careful in the future.

WHEN VANSHIDHAR CAME OUT OF THE COURT, HE WAS SHOWERED WITH VOLLEYS OF SARCASTIC COMMENTS FROM ALL SIDES.
Salute, sir!
Look at this man! He wanted to punish Pandit-ji. The court has wiped out all his arrogance!
Trying to be honest, huh? Did you get an award for it?
BUT EVERY HARSH WORD AND GESTURE ONLY FUELLED THE FLAMES OF HIS PRIDE. EVEN IF HE HAD WON THE CASE, HE MIGHT NOT HAVE WALKED WITH A PROUDER HEAD.
MUNSHI VANSHIDHAR WAS NOW REALISING THAT JUSTICE AND LEARNING, LOFTY TITLES, FLOWING BEARDS AND LOOSE GOWNS - NONE OF THESE DESERVED ANY RESPECT.

PANDIT ALOPIDIN CAME OUT SMILING. HIS NEAR AND DEAR ONES SHOWERED CURRENCY NOTES TO GREET HIM.

THE SEA OF GENEROSITY WAS ON A HIGH TIDE, AND ITS WAVES SHOOK THE VERY FOUNDATIONS OF JUSTICE.

VANSHIDHAR HAD ANTAGONISED ARTHA. HE HAD TO PAY THE PRICE FOR HIS RIGHTEOUSNESS. HARDLY A WEEK HAD PASSED WHEN HE RECEIVED A SUSPENSION LETTER. HE WAS REWARDED FOR CARRYING OUT HIS DUTY.
You are suspended!
BROKEN-HEARTED, SAD, BEWILDERED, THE POOR FELLOW HEADED HOME.

A FEW DAYS LATER, WHEN VANSHIDHAR RETURNED HOME IN THAT PITIABLE STATE AND THE OLD MAN HEARD THE NEWS, HE STARTED BEATING HIS HEAD.
Shall I break my head or yours?
HE SAID MANY HARSH WORDS, AND IF VANSHIDHAR HAD NOT REMOVED HIMSELF FROM HIS FATHER'S SIGHT, THE OLD MAN'S ANGER MIGHT HAVE ESCALATED.

HIS MOTHER WAS ALSO UNHAPPY. ALL HER PLANS OF PILGRIMAGE TO JAGANNATH AND RAMESHWARAM WERE GONE NOW.
HIS WIFE, TOO, WAS RESENTFUL AND DID NOT TALK TO HIM FOR DAYS.

The boy turned a deaf ear to all my advice and did whatever he pleased.
And now I have to deal with the barbs from the wine-seller and the butcher and live in deprivation in my old age. All we have is my meagre salary!
I have also been in service, holding a small rank, but I worked and worked hard.
And this man is parading his integrity.
Never mind the darkness at home, he insists on lighting a lamp at the mosque.
It's unbelievable. All this education has gone to waste.

A WEEK LATER, THE OLD MUNSHIJI WAS PRAYING ONE EVENING.
JUST THEN, AN ORNAMENTAL CHARIOT STOPPED AT HIS DOOR.
MUNSHIJI WENT OUTSIDE TO GREET THE VISITOR, WHO TURNED OUT TO BE PANDIT ALOPIDIN. MUNSHIJI LOWERED HIS HEAD IN SALUTATION AND BEGAN WITH A PROFUSE DISPLAY OF ADMIRATION
It is our good fortune to see you at our doorstep. You are like a god to us.
How can I show you my face, which has been smeared with disgrace? But what can I do? My son is an unlucky black sheep.

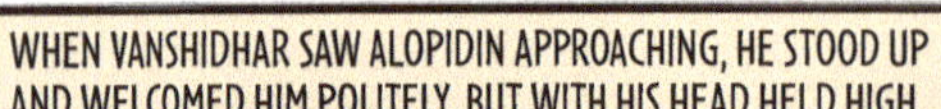

WHEN VANSHIDHAR SAW ALOPIDIN APPROACHING, HE STOOD UP AND WELCOMED HIM POLITELY, BUT WITH HIS HEAD HELD HIGH.

HE BELIEVED THIS MAN HAD COME TO FURTHER INSULT AND HUMILIATE HIM.

Inspector sahib, please do not consider this flattery. I haven't travelled this far just to flatter you.
That day, you arrested me with your authority, but today, I've come willingly to be arrested by you.
I've enslaved them all with my wealth. You alone had the guts to vanquish me. Allow me to say something.
I've encountered thousands of rich and wealthy people, and interacted with numerous high-ranking officials.
You did not accept my request at the river bank. But today I must insist that you do.
I may not be of much use to you, but I will do my utmost to serve you.

Accept this position and sign here. I am a Brahmin, and will not leave until you agree to this.
You want to appoint me as the manager of all your properties?
Yes! Along with a salary of six thousand rupees per annum, additional daily expenses, a horse to ride, a bungalow to live in and servants to serve you!

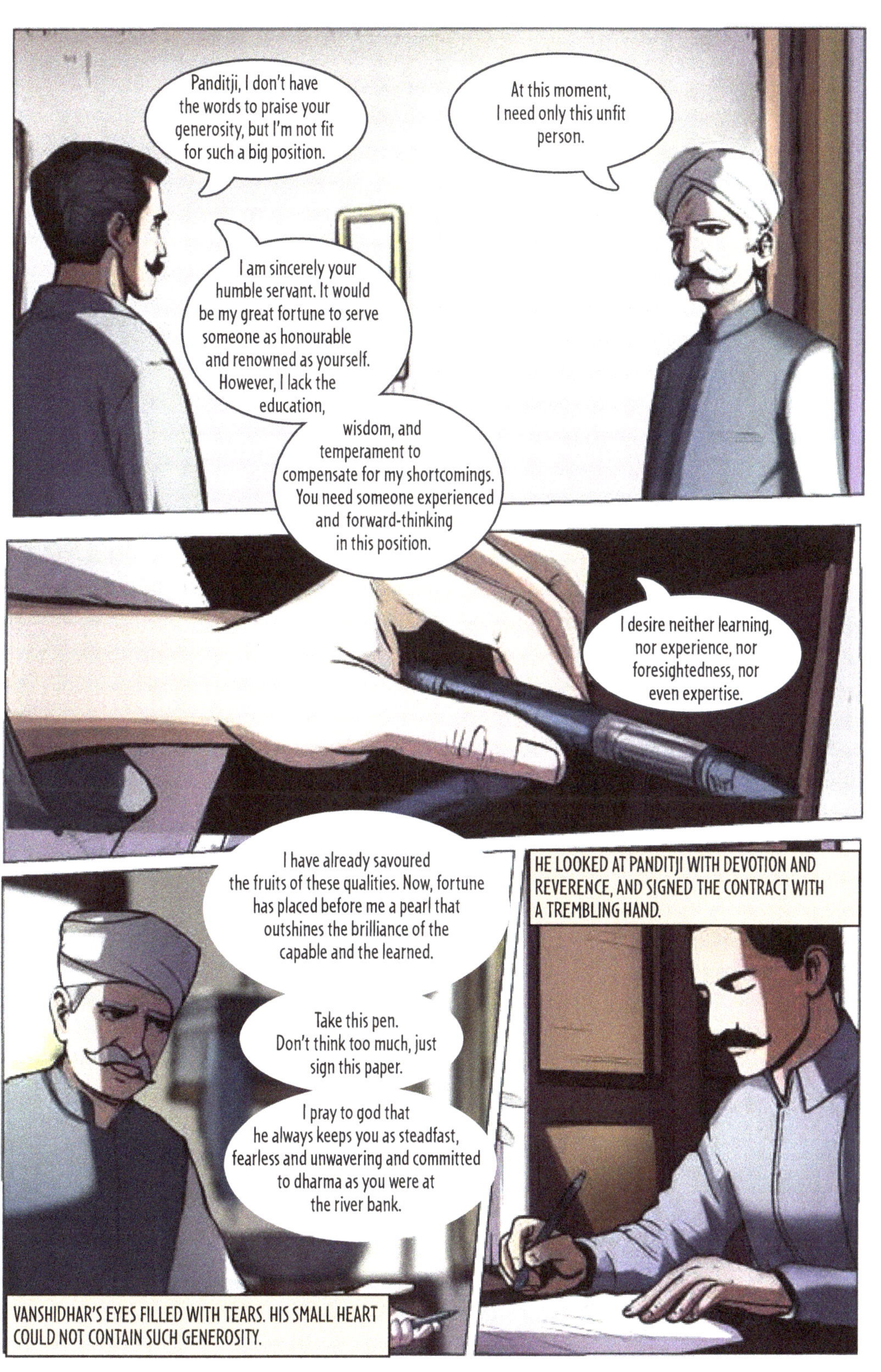

Panditji, I don't have the words to praise your generosity, but I'm not fit for such a big position.
At this moment, I need only this unfit person.
I am sincerely your humble servant. It would be my great fortune to serve someone as honourable and renowned as yourself. However, I lack the education,
wisdom, and temperament to compensate for my shortcomings. You need someone experienced and forward-thinking in this position.
I desire neither learning, nor experience, nor foresightedness, nor even expertise.
I have already savoured the fruits of these qualities. Now, fortune has placed before me a pearl that outshines the brilliance of the capable and the learned.
Take this pen. Don't think too much, just sign this paper.
I pray to god that he always keeps you as steadfast, fearless and unwavering and committed to dharma as you were at the river bank.
HE LOOKED AT PANDITJI WITH DEVOTION AND REVERENCE, AND SIGNED THE CONTRACT WITH A TREMBLING HAND.
VANSHIDHAR'S EYES FILLED WITH TEARS. HIS SMALL HEART COULD NOT CONTAIN SUCH GENEROSITY.

EIDGAH

EID ARRIVES AFTER THIRTY DAYS OF RAMADAN, THE MONTH OF FASTING. HOW WONDERFUL AND BEAUTIFUL IT IS, THIS MORNING OF EID!

THE SKY HAS A LOVELY PINK GLOW. THE TREES LOOK GREENER, THE FIELDS MORE FESTIVE.

LOOK AT THE SUN! IT RISES THIS MORNING BRIGHTER AND MORE DAZZLING THAN BEFORE TO WISH THE WORLD A VERY HAPPY EID.

THE VILLAGE IS ABUZZ WITH EXCITEMENT. EVERYONE IS UP EARLY TO GO TO THE MOSQUE.

Run along and get some thread and a needle from the neighbours. There's a button missing on your shirt.
The leather of my shoes has become as stiff as board. I have to run to the oil-press to get them greased.
I'm feeding the cows early today. We don't want to be late for prayers at the Eidgah. It's a good three miles away from the village.
There will be hundreds of people to greet and chat with. We will certainly not be done before midday.

The boys are the most excited. I heard that some of them kept only one fast, and that only till noon.

Haha! And some didn't even do that.

But no one can deny them the joy of going to the Eidgah. Fasting is for the grown-ups and the aged.

Oh yes, for the boys, only the day of Eid matters. They haven't been able to talk about anything else for weeks!

AT LONG LAST, THE DAY HAS COME.
Ammi! Hurry up!
Don't be so impatient!
Haha! I just can't wait to eat the pudding, Ammi.
THE BOYS HAVE NO INTEREST AT ALL IN ALL THE NITTY-GRITTY OF ARRANGEMENTS AND DETAILS. ALL THEY WANT IS TO EAT THE VERMICELLI PUDDING.
THEY HAVE NO IDEA WHY ABBAJAN IS RUNNING TO CHAUDHARY KARIM ALI'S HOUSE. OR THAT THE CHAUDHARY COULD TURN THEIR BIG DAY INTO A DAY OF MOURNING.
THE KIDS' POCKETS ARE BULGING WITH COINS. THEY REPEATEDLY TAKE THE TREASURE OUT OF THEIR POCKETS, COUNT AND RECOUNT IT BEFORE PUTTING IT BACK.
One ... two ... ten ... twelve. I have twelve pice.
One ... two ... three ... eight ... nine ... fifteen pice.
WITH THIS MONEY, THEY PLAN TO PURCHASE ALL KINDS OF ITEMS: TOYS, SWEETS, PAPER PIPES, RUBBER BALLS AND MUCH MORE.

NO ONE IS HAPPIER THAN HAMID THAT EID IS FINALLY HERE. HE IS ONLY FOUR – POORLY DRESSED, THIN AND FAMISHED-LOOKING.
HIS FATHER DIED OF CHOLERA LAST YEAR.
HIS MOTHER ALSO PASSED AWAY SOON AFTER. NO ONE KNEW WHAT HAD AILED HER.
NOW, HAMID SLEEPS IN HIS GRANDMOTHER AMEENA'S LAP, AND IS HAPPY WITH JUST THAT.

HAMID'S MIND IS BRIMMING WITH HAPPY THOUGHTS.
When my father comes back with sacks full of silver and mother brings back gifts from Allah, I will be able to fulfil all my heart's desires.
Then I will have more than Mahmood, Mohsin, Noorey and Sammi.
IT IS GREAT TO LIVE ON HOPE; FOR A CHILD, THERE IS NOTHING LIKE HOPE. A CHILD'S IMAGINATION CAN CREATE A MIGHTY MOUNTAIN OUT OF A TINY MOLEHILL.
HAMID HAS NO SHOES ON HIS FEET; THE CAP ON HIS HEAD IS SOILED AND TATTERED; ITS GOLD THREAD HAS TURNED BLACK. BUT HE IS HAPPY.

UNFORTUNATE AMEENA SHEDS TEARS IN HER DINGY LITTLE ROOM.

It is Eid and I do not have even a handful of grain. If only my Abid were here, it would have been a different kind of Eid!

Granny, don't you fret over me! I will be the first to get back. Don't worry!

Other boys are going out with their fathers. I am the only 'father' Hamid has.

How can I let him go to the fair all by himself? What if he gets lost in the crowd? No, I must not lose my precious little boy!

Hamid, how can you walk three miles?

I can, granny.

He doesn't even have a pair of shoes. He will get blisters on his feet.

If I went along, him I could pick him up now and then.
But then I need to collect ingredients for the vermicelli.
If only I had the money, I could have bought the ingredients on the way back and quickly made the pudding.
Please, granny, let me go.
Okay, go, but be careful.
THE VILLAGERS LEAVE IN ONE BIG PARTY. HAMID WALKS WITH THE BOYS. THEY OFTEN RUN AHEAD OF THE ELDERS, AND THEN WAIT FOR THEM IN THE SHADE UNDER A TREE.
Why do the oldies drag their feet?

THEY REACH THE OUTSKIRTS OF THE TOWN. ON BOTH SIDES OF THE ROAD ARE MANSIONS OF THE RICH ENCLOSED BY THICK, HIGH WALLS ON EVERY SIDE.
Look! The mango and lychee trees are laden with fruit.
Hahahaha
Who threw the stone!
What a silly ass we made of the gardener!

THE BOYS KEEP MOVING. THEY REACH THE SWEETMEAT VENDORS' STORES, WHICH ARE DECORATED WITH PILES OF DELICACIES.
My Abba says that, at midnight, there is a jinn at every stall. He has all that remains weighed, and pays in real rupees, just the sort of rupees we have.
Where would the jinns come by rupees?
Jinns are never short of money. They can get their hands on any treasure they want!
How do people make jinns happy?
I do not know, but Chaudhary Sahib has a lot of jinns under his control. If anything is stolen, he can trace it and even name the thief.
Jinns tell him everything that is going on in the world.

EVENTUALLY, THEY REACH THE EIDGAH. THERE ARE ROWS UPON ROWS OF WORSHIPPERS AS FAR AS THE EYE CAN SEE, SPILLING WELL BEYOND THE MOSQUE COURTYARD.

HAMID AND HIS FRIENDS WASH THEIR HANDS AND FEET, AND MAKE THEIR OWN LINE BEHIND THE OTHERS.

HERE, NEITHER WEALTH NOR STATUS MATTERS BECAUSE, IN THE EYES OF ISLAM, ALL MEN ARE EQUAL.

SUCH A BEAUTIFUL, STIRRING SIGHT! HOW PERFECTLY THEIR MOVEMENTS COORDINATE! LOOK AT THOSE HUNDRED THOUSAND HEADS BOWING TOGETHER IN PRAYER!

THE PRAYER IS OVER. MEN EMBRACE EACH OTHER.
THE BOYS RUN OFF TO LAUNCH AN ATTACK ON THE SWEET AND TOY VENDORS' STORES.

Let's go on the ride!
Sure thing!

Give us tickets, please!

HAMID WATCHES THEM FROM A DISTANCE.
All I have are three pice. I can't afford to part with a third of this treasure for a few miserable rounds.

HIS FRIENDS ARE NOW DONE WITH THE MERRY-GO-ROUNDS; IT IS TIME FOR TOYS NOW. THERE IS A ROW OF STALLS ON ONE SIDE SELLING ALL KINDS OF TOYS.

MOHSIN BUYS A POLICEMAN, WHILE MAHMOOD BUYS A LAWYER.

BUT HAMID DOESN'T BUY ANYTHING.

The toys are made of clay. One fall and they'll break into pieces. But I wish I could hold them for just a moment or two ...
My policeman will guard my house. If a thief comes near, he will shoot him with his gun.
HAMID STRETCHES OUT HIS HANDS, BUT STOPS A LITTLE SHORT
GRAB
BUT YOUNG BOYS ARE NOT GIVERS, PARTICULARLY WHEN IT IS SOMETHING NEW. POOR HAMID DOESN'T GET TO TOUCH THE TOYS.
Hey! Don't touch my policeman.
AFTER THE TOYS, THE BOYS HEAD TO THE STALLS SELLING SWEETS. THEY SMACK THEIR LIPS WITH RELISH AS THEY BUY SESAME SEED CANDY, GULAB JAMUNS OR HALWA. ONLY HAMID IS LEFT OUT. THE LUCKLESS BOY HAS ONLY THREE PICE. HE LOOKS WITH HUNGRY EYES AT THE OTHERS.

Hamid, why aren't you buying anything? Don't you like sweets?
What is so special about sweets? The books all say that they are bad for your health.
Why won't you part with the money in your pocket?
I know what this clever fellow is up to. When we've spent all our money, he will buy sweets and tease us.

Well, Hamid, your plan isn't going to work with us.
Yumm!
It's so tasty! Do you see this, Hamid?
SLURP SLURP

I don't care for your sweets.
Oh! My granny does not have a pair of tongs. Each time she roasts chapattis, the iron plate burns her hands.
WHILE THE OTHER CHILDREN MOVE AHEAD, HAMID STOPS BY A STALL THAT IS SELLING A PILE OF TONGS.

If I buy her a pair of tongs, she will never burn her fingers again.

Of what use are toys? They are a waste of money. You can have some fun with them, but only for a very short time. Then you forget all about them.
If I buy the tongs, the whole village will be saying, 'Hamid has bought his granny a pair of tongs, how nice he is!'
No one will bless the other boys for the toys they have bought themselves. I must buy these tongs.

AFTER SOME BARGAINING, HAMID BUYS THE TONGS FOR THREE PICE. HE CARRIES IT ON ONE SHOULDER AS IF IT WERE A GUN AND STRUTS UP PROUDLY TO SHOW IT TO HIS FRIENDS.

Are these tongs some kind of toy?
Of course! Place it across your shoulders and it is a gun. Wield it in your hands, and it is like the tongs carried by singing mendicants – it can make the sound of cymbals. One smack and it will reduce all your toys to dust.

THE PAIR OF TONGS WINS OVER EVERYONE. BUT NOW NO ONE HAS ANY MONEY LEFT, AND THE FAIRGROUND HAS BEEN LEFT FAR BEHIND.
DESPITE HIS FRIENDS' EARLIER BEHAVIOUR, HAMID HAS NO HESITATION IN SHARING HIS TONGS, WHICH THEY PASS FROM ONE HAND TO ANOTHER. AND THE TOYS ARE IN TURN HANDED TO HAMID.

HAMID'S FRIENDS START TO UNDERSTAND THAT HAMID'S TONGS POSSESS A DIFFERENT KIND OF POWER AND CHARM. THEIR EARLIER DISAPPROVAL TURNS INTO ADMIRATION.

BY ELEVEN, THE VILLAGE IS BUZZING WITH EXCITEMENT. THE FAIRGOERS HAVE RETURNED HOME.

Brother!

SNATCH
Don't do that! It's mine!

SLIP

SHATTER

MEANWHILE, HAMID'S GRANDMOTHER IS EAGERLY WAITING FOR HIS RETURN.
Wekome back, dear!
Look what I got, Amma!
Where did you find those tongs?
I bought it for you.

AMEENA'S ANGER QUICKLY MELTS INTO LOVE AND ADMIRATION FOR HER GRANDSON'S BEAUTIFUL GESTURE OF CONCERN FOR HER. HER HEART FEELS LIKE IT WOULD BURST WITH LOVE FOR THIS CHILD AND HIS SELFLESSNESS.

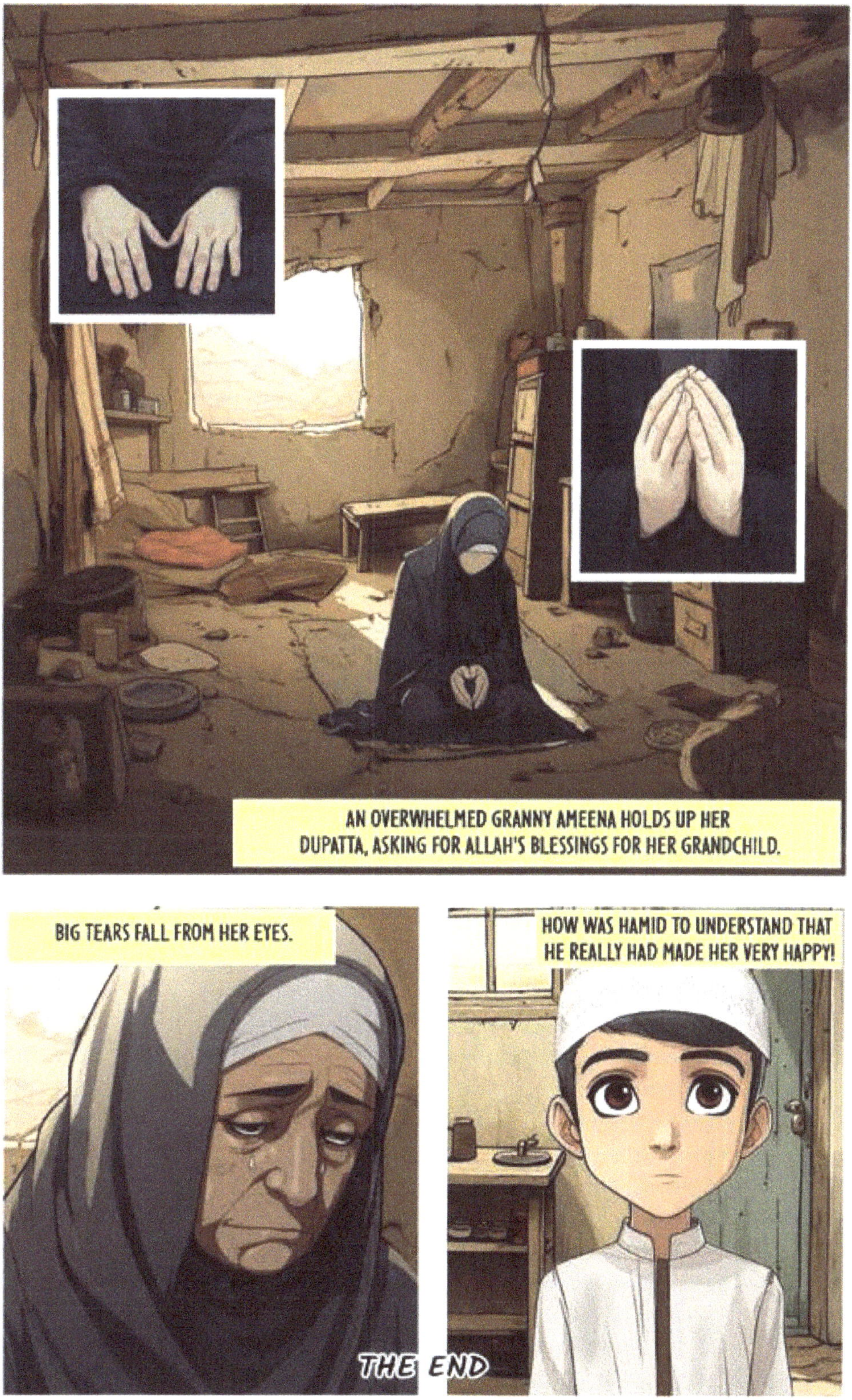

AN OVERWHELMED GRANNY AMEENA HOLDS UP HER DUPATTA, ASKING FOR ALLAH'S BLESSINGS FOR HER GRANDCHILD.

THE END